ALL YEAR ROUND

Winter

by
Emilie Dufresne

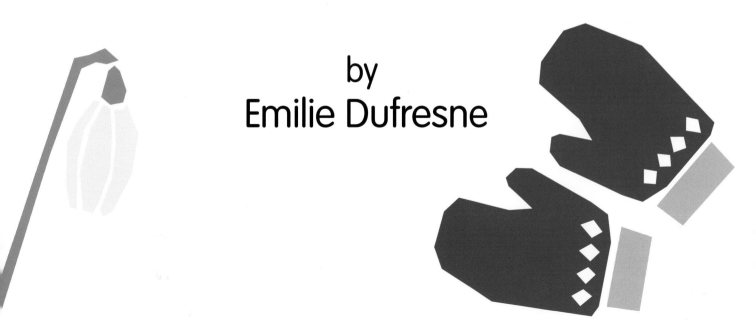

BookLife
PUBLISHING

©2018
BookLife Publishing
King's Lynn
Norfolk PE30 4LS

A catalogue record for this book is available from the British Library.

ISBN: 978-1-78637-405-9

Written by:

Emilie Dufresne

Edited by:

Holly Duhig

Designed & Illustrated by:

Danielle Jones

IMAGE CREDITS

Cover – Ami Parikh. 4 – Inara Prusakova. 5 – kdshutterman. 6 – Anna Grigorjeva. 7 – V. Belov. 8 – ANURAK PONGPATIMET. 10 – Giusparta. 11 – Samot. 12 – esthermm. 14 – Ruslan Guzov. 15 – MaraZe. 16 – Tomsickova Tatyana. 18 – windu. 19 –Aleksey Sagitov. 20 – Coatesy 22–23 – mandritoiu. Illustrations by Danielle Jones. Images are courtesy of Shutterstock.com. With thanks to Getty Images, Thinkstock Photo and iStockphoto.

CONTENTS

Words that look like <u>this</u> can be found in the glossary on page 24.

It's Winter!

Brr! It's cold outside! The days are short and the nights are dark. It must be… winter!

Winter is a season of the year. Seasons change when the weather changes. Every season is different.

Summer

Autumn

Spring

Winter

5

Winter Weather

In winter, the weather gets colder.
Sometimes it snows in winter!

The days in winter get shorter and shorter.
In some places, it is dark for the whole day.

IN SOME
COUNTRIES,
THIS HELPS YOU
TO SEE THE
NORTHERN
LIGHTS!

Winter Clothes

WHAT EXTRA LAYERS IS THIS BOY WEARING?

We need lots of clothes in winter.
Lots of layers help to keep you warm.

Snow is cold and wet. There are special clothes to wear in the snow.

Scarf

Gloves

Hat

Coat

WEARING WATERPROOF CLOTHES KEEPS YOU DRY.

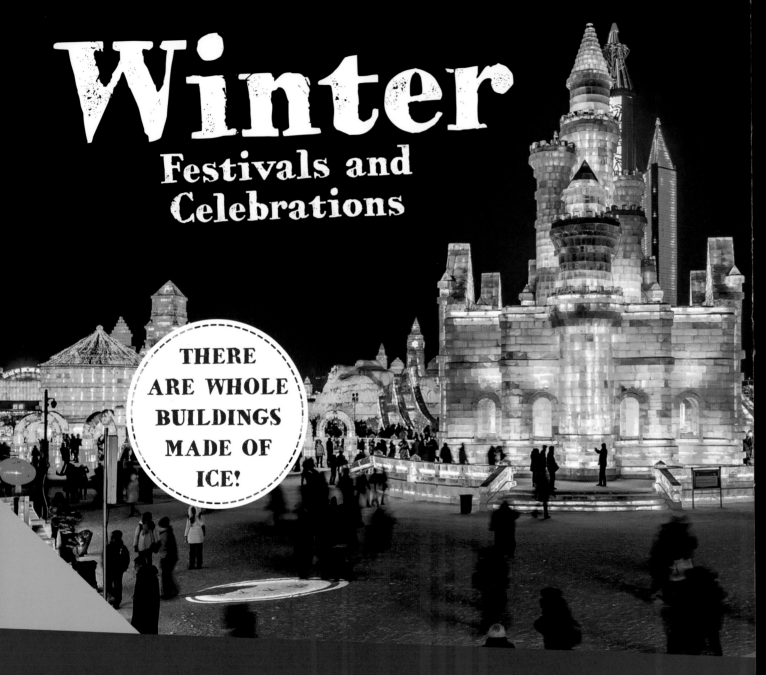

Winter
Festivals and Celebrations

THERE ARE WHOLE BUILDINGS MADE OF ICE!

In China people celebrate the Snow and Ice Festival. Big ice <u>sculptures</u> are made.

During winter in Venice, people dress up in old-fashioned clothes and masks.

WHAT IS YOUR FAVOURITE MASK?

Christians celebrate Christmas during winter. It is a <u>religious</u> holiday. People sing Christmas carols.

At Christmas, some people eat mince pies.
They are sweet pastries filled with fruit.

THERE'S NOT REALLY ANY MINCED MEAT IN THERE!

Sweet Pastry

Dried Fruits

13

Winter Food

WHAT KINDS OF SOUP HAVE YOU TRIED?

Eating soup is a great way to keep warm in winter.

Lots of root vegetables are <u>in season</u> during winter.

Celeriac

Turnips

Onions

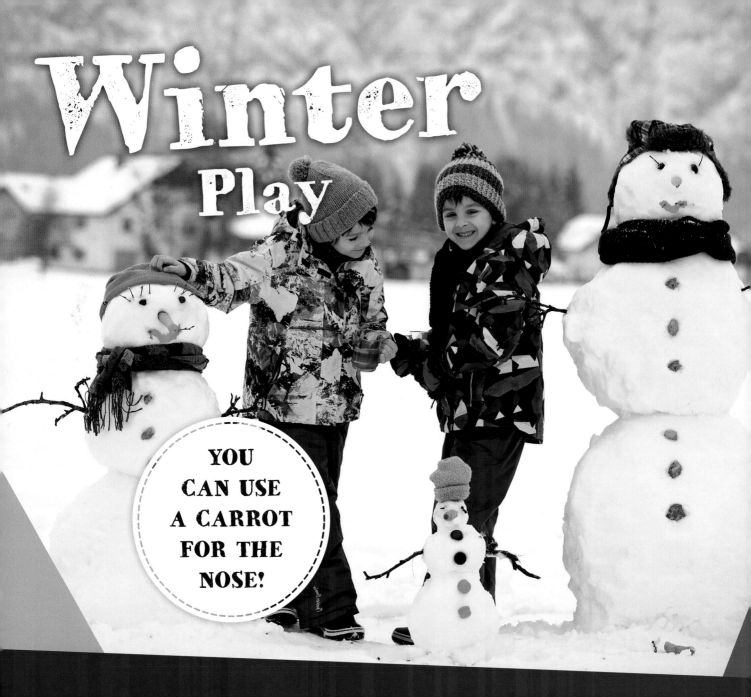

Winter
Play

YOU
CAN USE
A CARROT
FOR THE
NOSE!

There are lots of fun things to do in winter.
If it snows, you can build a snowman.

In winter, there are lots of places to go ice skating.

WATCH OUT!
ICE IS VERY
SLIPPERY!

Plants in Winter

TREES THAT KEEP THEIR LEAVES ARE CALLED EVERGREENS.

Some plants lose their leaves in the winter. Other plants keep their leaves all year round.

Some flowers can stay alive even in very cold weather. Snowdrops can grow out of the snow.

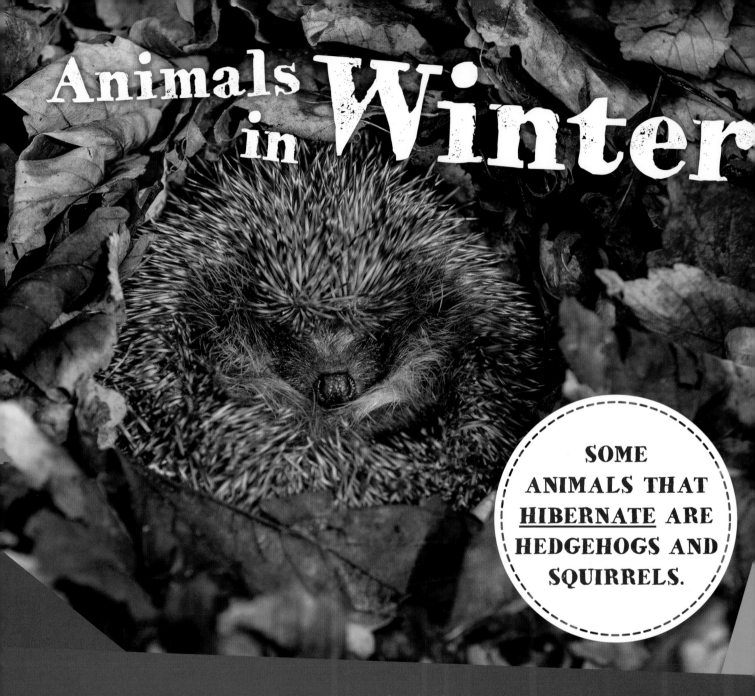

Animals in Winter

In winter some animals hibernate. They go into a deep sleep and their bodies slow down.

Bats also hibernate. They can go into a very deep sleep.

WHEN HIBERNATING, BATS MIGHT ONLY BREATHE ONCE AN HOUR!

21

What Comes Next?

As winter comes to an end, the weather gets warmer and daytime gets longer.

Winter is becoming... spring!

GLOSSARY

hibernate   when an animal or plant spends the winter sleeping

in season   when a plant grows best

northern lights   a natural wonder where bands of light appear in the sky near the North Pole

religious   relating to, or believing in, a religion

sculptures   statues and objects made by carving materials

waterproof   something water cannot pass through

INDEX

24